Kids' Guide to
PADDLING

ALL YOU NEED TO KNOW ABOUT HAVING FUN WHILE PADDLING

By Tom Watson

This library edition published in 2018 by Walter Foster Jr.,
an imprint of The Quarto Group
6 Orchard Road, Suite 100
Lake Forest, CA 92630

Written by Tom Watson

The National Wildlife Federation & Ranger Rick contributors:
Children's Publication Staff, Licensing Staff, and in-house naturalist David Mizejewski.

Photographs © Shutterstock, except pages 8, 10-11, 12, 13 (top two images),
17-18, 19 (bottom two images), 20, 40, 48-49, 52, © Tom Watson; 58, 59 (bottom)
© SeaLine; 61 © Lena Conlan.

Distributed in the United States and Canada by
Lerner Publisher Services
241 First Avenue North
Minneapolis, MN 55401 U.S.A.
www.lernerbooks.com

First Library Edition

Library of Congress Cataloging-in-Publication Data

Names: Watson, Tom, 1947- author.
Title: Ranger Rick kids' guide to paddling : all you need to know about
   having fun while paddling / By Tom Watson.
Description: Lake Forest, CA : Quarto Publishing Group, 2018. | Includes
   index. | Audience: Age 8. | Audience: Grade 4 to 6.
Identifiers: LCCN 2018006223 | ISBN 9781942875765 (hardcover : alk. paper)
Subjects: LCSH: Kayaking--Juvenile literature. | Canoes and
   canoeing--Juvenile literature.
Classification: LCC GV784.3 .W38 2018 | DDC 797.122/4--dc23
LC record available at https://lccn.loc.gov/2018006223

Printed in USA
9 8 7 6 5 4 3 2 1

TABLE OF CONTENTS

Ranger Rick

If you're like most kids who love the outdoors, you also love kayaking, canoeing, or paddle-boarding! By reading this book, you'll learn all about small watercraft and how to paddle them, what gear to take with you on the water, beautiful places to paddle, and also what wildlife to look out for on the water. You'll find lots of great tips, like how to paddle comfortably so you can paddle for hours, and techniques for going forward, backward, and sideways, all without getting wet!

The better you get at the skills taught in this book, the more fun you'll have on your next paddling adventure! So read the tips, and then head for the great outdoors to practice.

Happy paddling!

Ranger Rick

CANOE OR KAYAK?

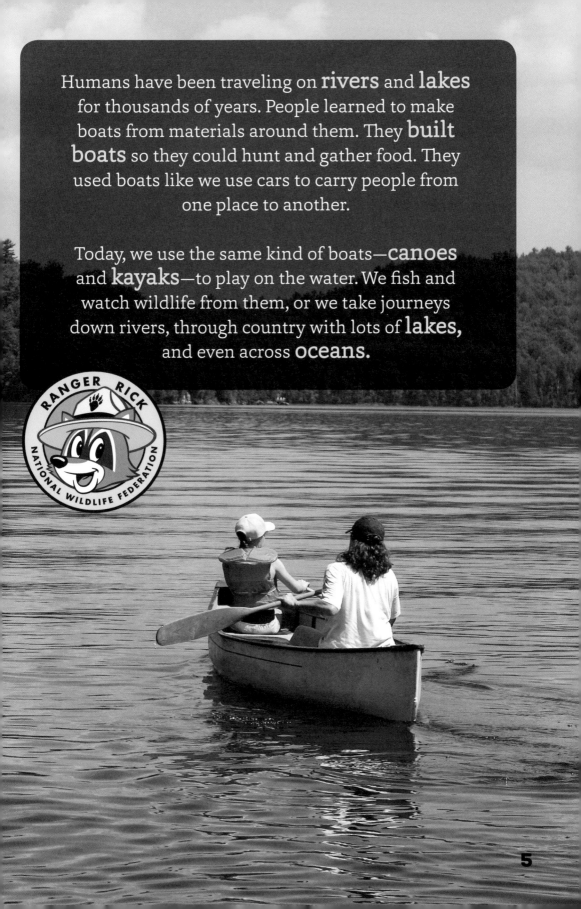

Humans have been traveling on **rivers** and **lakes** for thousands of years. People learned to make boats from materials around them. They **built boats** so they could hunt and gather food. They used boats like we use cars to carry people from one place to another.

Today, we use the same kind of boats—**canoes** and **kayaks**—to play on the water. We fish and watch wildlife from them, or we take journeys down rivers, through country with lots of **lakes,** and even across **oceans.**

CANOES

The first canoes were made from carved-out tree trunks and called dugout canoes. Many of the different kinds of canoes we use today are like the skin boats built by the first inhabitants of the North Pacific area. They used skins of animals to cover a frame made from trees and animal bones.

Some American Indian tribes built boats using the bark from birch trees. They tore the bark off the tree in sheets and used it to cover the frame. Thread made from animal intestines was used to help sew the bark together. Sap from trees was made into a waterproof glue.

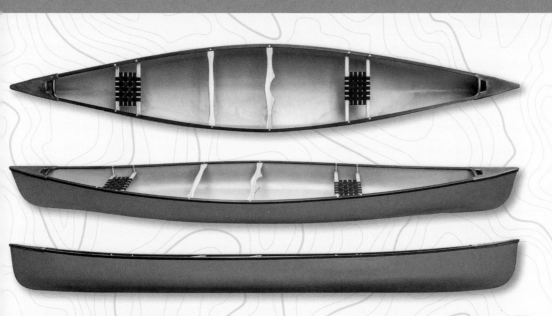

Today, strips of wood from cedar and ash trees are popular for making strip canoes. Canoes can also be built from man-made materials such as aluminum, plastic, fiberglass, and graphite. These canoes come in many different colors.

PARTS OF A CANOE

The front is called the **bow**. The back is called the **stern**. The center of the boat is called the **midsection**.

The edge or rim around the top of the canoe is called the **gunwale** (pronounced "gunnel"). The pieces that stretch across the canoe are **thwarts**. The gunwale and thwarts help the canoe keep its shape and add strength.

Some canoes have a special thwart in the middle called a **yoke**. The yoke has a shallow "U" formed into it. The yoke fits around your neck and lets you more easily carry the canoe on your shoulders.

Where lakes and rivers are separated by short sections of land, you must carry your canoe from one body of water, to another. Carrying your canoe over land is called a **portage** or **portaging**.

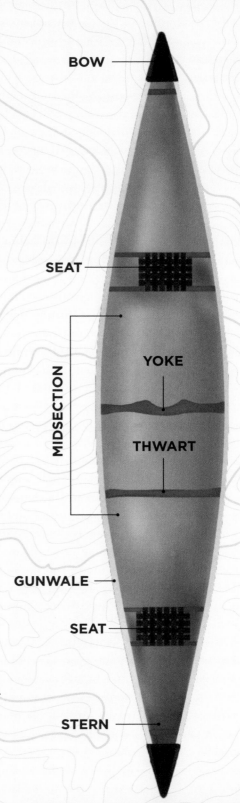

BOW

SEAT

MIDSECTION

YOKE

THWART

GUNWALE

SEAT

STERN

Many canoes have bench-like seats covered in webbing. Others have a seat that looks like the seat on a tractor. It is molded to fit the shape of your rear end. Some people like the molded seat because it is more comfortable. It also helps you sit straight and slightly forward to paddle.

Bench seat covered in webbing

Molded seat

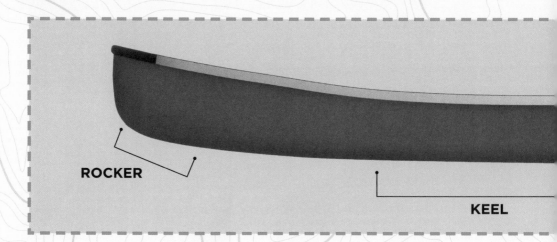

ROCKER

KEEL

The ends of the canoe are called **stems**. A high stem usually means a drier ride because it protects you from the water splashing up over the bow or stern. If you want to know how deep a canoe is, you measure it from the middle of the canoe.

The center line along the length of the bottom of the canoe is called the **keel**. It runs all along the boat from the bow to the stern. If you place a canoe on flat ground, it may lie flat all along the keel or it may curve up away from the ground at each end. That curve is called **rocker**.

A canoe with a flat keel is designed to go straight. Canoes that go straight without much effort are said to "track" well. These canoes are best used on open water where long, straight distances are paddled. Canoes with rocker are most often used on rivers where there are lots of turns to make and many obstacles to avoid. A canoe with rocker can turn more quickly and be maneuvered more easily. A canoe used in rapids and on very fast, white water of a river has a lot of rocker.

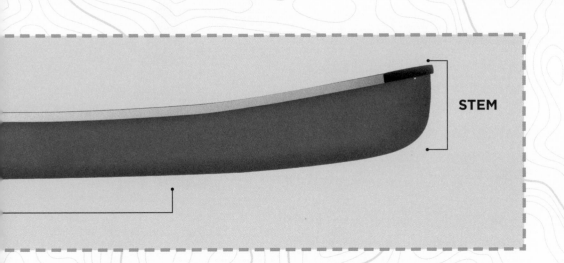

STEM

On an upside-down canoe, the keel is easy to see. It is the line running along the center of the boat.

CANOE OR KAYAK?

SIZE AND SHAPE

The average length of a canoe is about 16 feet (5 m).

Most canoes are between 30 and 36 inches (76 and 91 cm) wide depending on how long they are.

Canoes made of aluminum and some plastics can weigh more than 60 pounds (27 kg). New materials are being used to make canoes that are the same size but much lighter. Some weigh less than 40 pounds (18 kg)!

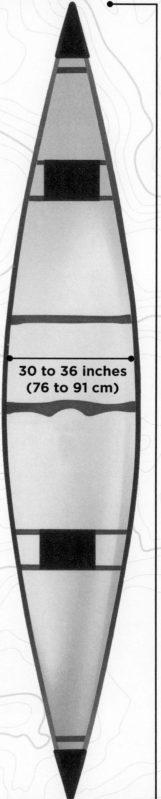

16 feet (5 m)

30 to 36 inches (76 to 91 cm)

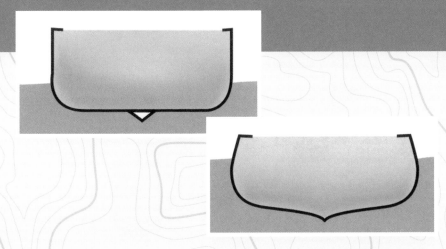

The cross section of some canoes at the widest part have flat bottoms; others are slightly "V" shaped. The flat bottom makes a very stable boat that can carry a lot of gear. In the photograph below, these paddlers keep their gear in the middle. A canoe with a slightly arched bottom can actually be more stable as it carries more weight. The part of the boat down in the water becomes wider and makes the boat more stable.

TYPES AND USES

Canoes used on rivers are often shorter than those used on the open water of lakes. Sometimes very tight turns are needed to go around bends in the river or to avoid rocks and trees in the water. A short canoe can turn quicker and easier than a longer canoe.

Specially designed canoes are used for racing down rivers, across lakes, or over great distances on the ocean. A racing canoe can be very tippy.

Wide boats are usually more stable. Because they are usually shorter, they turn better than the narrow boats, but they are harder to keep straight.

Some boats are built for just one paddler. The sides on these "solo" canoes are usually turned in so the boat is narrower where the paddler sits. This is called **tumblehome**, making it so the paddler doesn't have to reach out as far to paddle correctly.

Most canoes are designed to carry two paddlers. Longer canoes can usually carry a third person instead of extra gear. Some boats that are designed for one person can also be paddled by two smaller paddlers. There are some smaller two-person canoes that can be easily paddled by one larger paddler.

If you want to carry a lot of gear, a longer canoe is better than a wider one because it will usually track better, too.

KAYAKS

A kayak is very similar to a canoe in many ways. It, too, comes to a point at the front and the back and is moved through the water by one or two paddlers. Kayaks come in a variety of shapes and lengths. Like canoes, they are designed to perform in special ways on the water.

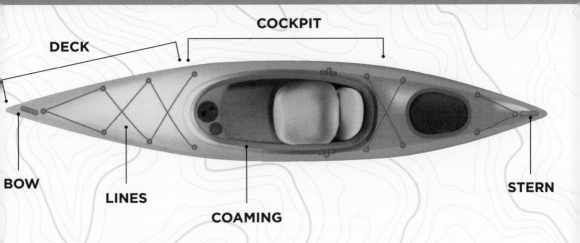

COCKPIT

DECK

BOW

LINES

COAMING

STERN

PARTS OF A KAYAK

Some parts of the kayak and canoe have the same names: the front of the boat is called the **bow,** the rear is called the **stern**. The center line down the middle of the bottom of the boat is called the **keel**. What makes each boat special are the differences between them.

A kayak has a deck that covers the top of the boat. In the center of the deck is a hole. This is called the **cockpit**. It is where the paddler sits. Some people use a special cover for this cockpit, which is called a **spray skirt**. It fits snugly around the waist of the paddler and then attaches to the rim of the cockpit (called the **coaming**). The spray skirt keeps water from getting inside the kayak. This keeps the boat dry and lets the paddler use the kayak even when the water is rough and washing up over the deck of the boat.

The deck has special **lines** attached to it. These are lengths of cord attached to the boat to help hold things on deck. Because the deck can be very slippery when wet, lines also help a paddler hold onto the kayak from the water.

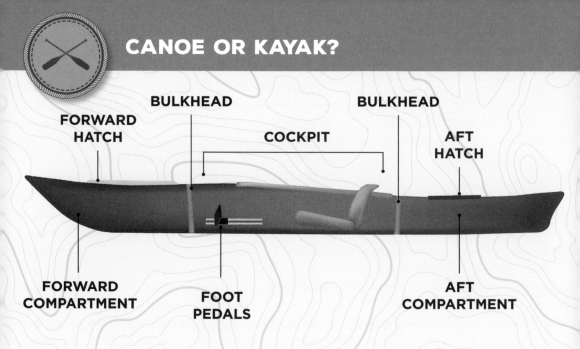

FORWARD
HATCH

BULKHEAD

COCKPIT

BULKHEAD

AFT
HATCH

FORWARD
COMPARTMENT

FOOT
PEDALS

AFT
COMPARTMENT

Because a kayak is covered by a deck, there is dry space inside the boat to carry gear and personal belongings. To reach inside the boat, kayaks have openings on the deck called **hatches**. The hatch has a waterproof cover so the inside stays dry.

The area inside the hatch is called a **compartment**. The compartment is separated from the rest of the inside of the boat by a wall called a **bulkhead**. The compartment in the front of the kayak is called the **forward compartment**. The one behind the cockpit is called the **aft compartment**.

A kayak usually has a **handle** near the bow and the stern of the deck. This handle makes it easier to carry the kayak to and from the water.

Many kayaks have either a **rudder** or a **skeg** to help keep the boat on course. A rudder swings back and forth and is moved using **foot pedals** inside the cockpit. A skeg is like a rudder blade, except it only moves up and down, not side to side like a rudder. It is used to help the boat stay on a straight path through the water. The paddler can use a cable to lower the skeg down or to pull it back up.

DOWN POSITION

UP POSITION

SIZE AND SHAPE

Whitewater kayaks are the shortest boats; some are only about 5 feet (1.5 m) long. A kayak for one paddler is usually 16 feet (5 m) long and about 22 inches (56 cm) wide. Some kayaks made for ocean surfing are more than 20 feet (6 m) long.

Kayaks are usually very narrow. Even longer boats that can carry three people are rarely wider than 30 inches (76 cm).

Like canoes, the longer the kayak, the easier it is to track. Shorter kayaks are easier to maneuver. Kayaks are usually more stable as they get wider. Some kayaks of the same length can carry more gear than others because the body of the kayak is deeper. These are called **high-volume kayaks**.

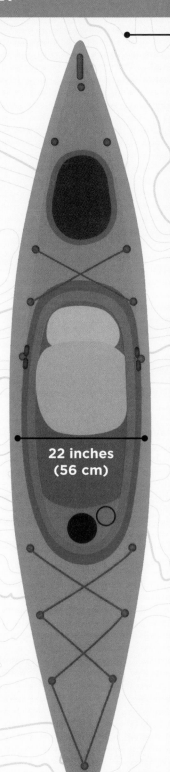

16 feet (5 m)

22 inches (56 cm)

In a canoe, the paddler can move around a lot, face different directions, and sit in different positions. In a kayak, the paddler has more contact with the boat. Good kayakers learn many ways to maneuver the kayak by leaning their body and sweeping with the paddle. A kayak is said to be "responsive" if it can be maneuvered easily.

A canoe can carry lots of gear, but a kayak has less room and usually carries less gear.

When placed side-by-side, a 16-foot (5 m) kayak is usually much narrower than a 16-foot (5 m) canoe. Because a kayak has a covered deck and sits lower in the water, it is usually easier to handle in rougher, windier weather than a canoe.

TYPES AND USES

Like canoes, kayaks that are shorter and wider are more stable. Most paddlers like to use them on calm and smooth water for fishing, photography, and relaxed paddling. They can be easy to maneuver but don't go as straight or paddle as easily as the longer, narrower kayaks.

Shorter kayaks that have bigger cockpits are called **recreational kayaks.** They are used more for playing in the water and not meant for long trips.

This experienced kayaker has a short whitewater kayak. He is also wearing a spray skirt, which fits over the cockpit once he sits in the boat. The spray skirt will keep him dry and secure him to the boat.

Longer, narrower kayaks that are used for taking trips on the ocean or across big lakes are called **touring kayaks.** They can hold a lot of gear. They usually track (go straight) better. They move fast through the water and with practice are easy to steer and control.

A popular type of kayak is the **whitewater boat.** This is the short, stubby boat you may see in rapids on a river. These boats are designed for paddling in very wild and crazy water. There are also canoes that are designed for paddling in white water, too.

Another kind of kayak looks like a fat surfboard. It is called a **Sit-On-Top kayak (SOT).** The paddler sits on the kayak instead of inside it. Because they are very stable and comfortable for beginning paddlers, these kayaks are very popular for fishing.

STAND-UP PADDLEBOARDING

You know all about canoes and kayaks, but they aren't the only things you can paddle! You may also want to try stand-up paddleboarding.

Stand-up paddleboarding (SUP) is a relatively new water sport that has become popular in recent years. Think of stand-up paddleboarding as a mixture between canoeing and surfing. You stand like you would on a surfboard and paddle like you would on a canoe.

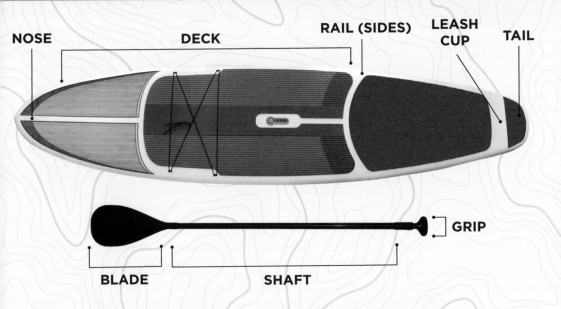

NOSE   DECK   RAIL (SIDES)   LEASH CUP   TAIL

GRIP

BLADE   SHAFT

PARTS OF A STAND-UP PADDLEBOARD

Like canoes and kayaks, SUPs have a **deck.** It's the part you stand on. The soft foam on top of the board is called a **deck pad.** The sides are called **rails.** The thicker the rails are, the more stable the board will be. SUPs also have **rockers,** just like canoes and kayaks.

The front of the board is called the **nose,** and the back is called the **tail.** On the tail, there is a **leash cup,** where the leash or tether is attached to the board. On the bottom, just like a surfboard, the SUP has **fins.** Fins make the paddleboard go straight more easily. SUPs also have handles to make them easier to carry.

SAFETY

Safety-minded stand-up paddleboarders wear life jackets and fasten the tether (leash) on their boards to their ankles. If you fall in, you will stay attached to your floating board. If you're not tethered, the board may float away quickly and leave you stranded in the water.

If you paddle out beyond a surfing or swimming area, know that there may be extra safety rules. The U.S. Coast Guard requires you to wear a personal flotation device (PFD), to bring a whistle to warn other boats of your location, and to bring a flashlight if you are out after sunset.

SIZE AND SHAPE

Stand-up paddleboards range from 9 to 15 feet (2.7 to 4.6 m) long, 30 to 56 inches (76 to 142 cm) wide, 4 to 8 inches (10 to 20 cm) thick, and weigh from 20 to 50 pounds (9 to 23 kg). They are all generally the same shape, like a surfboard. If you are new to SUP, bigger boards that are wider, longer, and thicker will be more stable and easier to use. Your paddle should be about 6 to 10 inches (15 to 25 cm) taller than you are.

TYPES AND USES

Most people like to leisurely paddle around and enjoy the scenery. But some people use SUPs to race, surf, or fish. Some even practice yoga on them.

There are many kinds of stand-up paddleboards. All-around SUPs are the most common type and good for beginners. Inflatable SUPs are easier to carry around and store. When deflated, they roll up to about the size of a sleeping bag. There are also SUPs designed for fishing, yoga, touring, surfing, and racing.

SUP boards can have one to four fins on the bottom. More fins help the board track better through the water. Just like canoes and kayaks, the shape of the SUP determines how it will handle in the water. Longer and skinnier SUPs are less stable and more challenging for beginners.

STAND-UP PADDLEBOARDING TIPS

Get a grip! Grab the "T" grip on the top of the paddle with one hand and the center of the shaft with your other hand. Make sure the blade (which is bent) angles forward and not backward. Bend your elbows and practice paddling. Just like with kayaking and canoeing, you will use your stomach and back muscles more than your arms.

Stay balanced. Make sure your knees aren't locked, and center your body over the board. If you want to turn, carefully take a step or two back on the board. If you feel yourself falling, try to fall away from the board so you don't hurt yourself.

WHAT GEAR DO I NEED?

If you enjoy spending your time on the water, your most important piece of equipment is your life jacket, or **PFD**. That stands for **Personal Flotation Device** because it is made to keep a person floating in the water. Even if you are a good swimmer, you should always wear a PFD when in a boat.

Depending on where and when you go paddling, you may wear special **clothing** and take **other gear.** Of course, you will need **paddles,** too!

LIFE JACKETS

A life jacket will keep you afloat if you get separated from your boat. It should be colorful so you can be seen easily in the water. It must fit well to work well, so get the right one for you. **Be sure you and your boating partners always wear life jackets!**

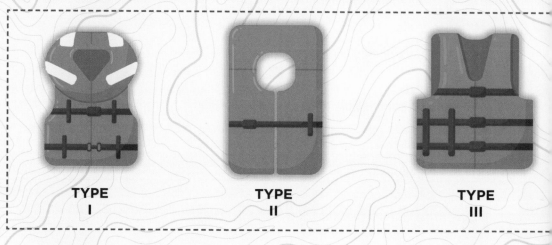

| TYPE I | TYPE II | TYPE III |

TYPES

Life jackets come in several different types. The personal flotation devices (PFDs) used by canoers and kayakers are called a **Type III**. It is designed to hold your head out of the water. **Type I** and **II** will actually turn you around so you float faceup, even when you are unconscious.

The jackets used by paddlers are compact. They need to be small and comfortable so the paddler can easily move around.

PROPER FIT

Besides being the right size and type, a good life jacket must fit well. If it's too tight, it won't be comfortable, and if it moves around, it may not keep you afloat properly. Adult jackets are usually sized in inches; kids' jackets are sized by age.

The easiest way to see if the life jacket fits properly is to put it on and pretend you are paddling your boat. Does the jacket give you enough room to move around and reach out for different parts of your make-believe boat? Does it pinch or poke you anywhere? Is it uncomfortable at all? If there is anything that doesn't feel right about your life jacket, try another one.

SAFETY

Life jackets used for canoeing are usually basic and often don't have all the "extras" found on a kayaking life jacket.

The extras on a kayaking life jacket include several pockets, straps, and loops so you can carry different types of small gear. Some of the items you might like to carry with you are a compass, a signaling whistle, a knife, and maybe some snacks, too. Be careful not to fill the pockets so full that they start to bulge out.

Gear hanging on the jacket, as well as overfilled pockets, can get caught on lines, coaming, and other parts of the deck. This can make it very hard or tiring to get back into the boat if you capsize.

Another important safety feature is the color of your life jacket. If you get separated from your boat, the color of your life jacket could help searchers find you.

Good colors for life jackets are bright yellow or orange, bright lime green and robin's-egg blue. Red may be an exciting color for racing cars and fire engines but it is not the best color for a PFD. It is hard to see at great distances, when it's really cloudy, or when the sun is low in the sky.

Another very important part of a good life jacket is a strip or patch of reflective tape. This tape reflects the light from a flashlight or spotlight and makes you easy to be seen even when it's too dark to see the entire boat.

Some life jackets have reflective patches on the panels in front and back and up on the top of the shoulder strap. If you have a life jacket that doesn't have reflective patches or stripes, you can buy reflective material in most marine hardware stores. It has a sticky backing on it to let you put it anywhere you want on your jacket.

The most important safety tip about any kind of boating is to **always wear your life jacket!**

CLOTHING AND ACCESSORIES

In general, you should wear clothing that is comfortable and quick drying. Be sure you know what the weather will be like when you go paddling. If it will be hot and sunny, you will want to protect your skin. If it will be cool, you will want to wear warmer clothing.

JACKETS, PANTS, AND BOOTS

If you paddle in cold water, you may want to wear a paddling jacket. It protects you from spray, from waves splashing against the boat, and even from water dripping off the paddle. Most paddling jackets have hoods, collars, cuffs, and waistbands that help keep water from getting inside your jacket.

Waterproof pants keep your bottom dry. Most of the time you can wear regular rain pants while paddling, especially when the water's cold.

Many paddlers don't wear shoes or boots at all. If you will be walking around in the water or on land, you might want some protection for your feet. Be sure you can still work the foot pedals.

HATS AND GLOVES

A lot of body heat is lost through the top of your head. Even if you don't like wearing a cap or a hat, you should bring one with you in case of sudden changes in the weather.

Hats for paddling are just like any other hats for the outdoors. They keep you warm or cool or dry. A good option is to wear a wide-brimmed hat with a flap on the back to cover your neck from the sun.

If your hands get wet while paddling, they can get cold very fast. Most paddlers carry gloves with them, even on warm summer days.

Another piece of equipment to keep hands dry and warm and to protect them from blisters is called a **pogie**. It is like a mitten for the paddle! It is attached to the paddle and has an opening at the wrist so you can push your hand into the pogie to grab the paddle shaft.

GEAR CHECKLIST

☐ **SUNGLASSES** The polarized type is best, so you can see through the glare on the surface of the water

☐ **NOSE PLUGS** You never know when you might capsize

☐ **SUNSCREEN** Sun reflecting off the water can give you a bad burn

☐ **EXTRA BATTERIES** Carry different sizes

☐ **BINOCULARS** Great for wildlife watching

☐ **COMPASS & CHARTS** Carry them in waterproof cases

☐ **CELL PHONE** Remember that some wilderness areas don't have service

☐ **FLASHLIGHT** Be sure it is waterproof

☐ **EXTRA MATCHES** Campfires are easier to start when dry matches are available

☐ **SIGNALING WHISTLE** It makes a very shrill sound to attract attention

☐ **BOATING KNIFE** The wavy teeth on the cutting edge can be used to cut through rope

☐ **THROW LINE** It can be tossed to a paddler in trouble

☐ **BILGE PUMP** Kayakers carry this small hand pump to remove water from their boat

☐ **DECK SPONGE** Good for wiping water, sand, and dust off your seat

☐ **BAILING BUCKET** Canoers often tie a bailing bucket onto one of the thwarts

☐ **DRY BAGS** They protect everything from getting wet

PADDLES

You are the motor of your canoe or kayak. The paddle makes the boat move forward or backward—even sideways! You use a paddle to move in all these directions, plus steer the boat. You also use it like a brake to stop the boat, or sometimes just to keep your balance on the water.

A paddle **shaft** is like your arm; the **blade** is like your hand. The blade of many paddles, especially those used for kayaking, is slightly curved—just like your hand while you are swimming.

PARTS OF A PADDLE

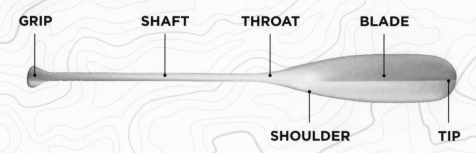

GRIP   SHAFT   THROAT   BLADE

SHOULDER   TIP

There are many things to consider when choosing the right paddle.

A canoe is usually paddled with just one blade. The blade is attached to one end of a short shaft. The other end is called the **grip.** It is where you grab the paddle to control the boat. Some solo canoers use a double kayak paddle with their canoes.

Kayak paddles have two blades at opposite ends of a long shaft. The outer end of the blade is called the **tip,** and the part that connects to the shaft is called the **throat.** The side of the blade that faces the paddler and is used to pull water is called the **power face.** Usually a double paddle, such as those used for kayaking, has flattened sections on the shaft. This is where the paddler grips the shaft and controls the paddle.

Kayak paddles come in one-piece or two-piece types. One advantage of a two-piece paddle is that you can take it apart for storage on your boat or at home.

PADDLE LENGTH

Canoe paddles are usually measured in inches. The average paddle is between 52 and 56 inches (132 to 142 cm) long.

Most kayak paddles are measured in centimeters (cm). The average length of a kayak touring paddle is between 220 and 230 cm (87 to 91 inches). A racing paddle might be as short as 205 to 210 cm (81 to 83 inches).

A canoe paddle has to be long enough so the paddler can reach out and place the entire blade in the water. If the paddle is too long, the entire blade and part of the shaft is in the water. If it's too short, the full surface of the blade is not working as well as it could.

BLADE SIZE AND SHAPE

Wide blades are used when a paddler wants a lot of power—either for a fast start or for quick, powerful maneuvers. Many racers choose a wide paddle blade.

A narrow blade is often the choice of those who like to use a light but steady stroke. Kayakers or canoers who enjoy a leisurely paddle on calm water just need enough power to keep their boats moving forward and in their control.

Paddles with the same shaft length can have different blade shapes and sizes.

Some blades have square ends, while others are rounded. One rounded blade is called the **beaver tail** because its shape is very much like the tail of the animal. A **bent-shaft** paddle looks broken because the blade meets the shaft at an angle. This design helps the paddler reach forward farther and faster to paddle more efficiently.

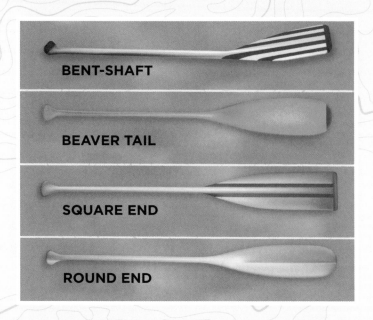

BENT-SHAFT

BEAVER TAIL

SQUARE END

ROUND END

Kayak blades, especially the wider ones, are usually curved from tip to throat and also from one edge to the other. Some used for racing have a deep curve, almost like a spoon. Others can be almost flat. The most common kayak paddle has a curve that looks very much like the curve of your hand while you are swimming.

A **Greenland paddle** was designed by kayakers in the country of Greenland. This paddle has very long, narrow blades at both ends of a short staff. They are usually made out of one long piece of wood.

A Greenland paddle

PADDLE MATERIAL

Both canoe and kayak paddles can be made of many different materials: wood, aluminum, and composite materials such as fiberglass and graphite. Those same materials are also used to make paddle blades. Lightweight but strong materials are used for long expeditions, competition, and other paddling where every bit of energy is needed.

DON'T FORGET THE SPARE!

Just like the spare tire carried in a car, a spare paddle is often carried by canoers and kayakers. Sometimes paddles break, and you wouldn't want to be out in the middle of a lake without any way of paddling back to shore.

Some paddlers like to have the same quality spare paddle as they have for everyday paddling. Others buy an inexpensive paddle to use in emergencies. A spare canoe paddle is much shorter and can usually be carried somewhere inside the canoe without being in the way. Kayakers usually use the two-piece paddle because it can come apart and be stowed (carried) on the deck of the kayak.

CANOE   PADDLEBOARD   KAYAK

WHICH SKILLS DO I NEED?

The more you **paddle,** the more comfortable you will feel in your canoe, kayak, or stand-up paddleboard. You will learn different ways to **steer your boat** and different ways of handling many challenging situations. The more you **practice,** the easier it will be to make **the boat feel like it is part of you.** That's the sign of a good paddler.

The best way to learn how to handle your boat is to learn and practice these three things: proper **posture,** good paddling **strokes,** and smooth **maneuvering** techniques.

POSTURE AND ENDURANCE

Good posture when paddling means sitting up straight in the canoe or kayak. Your rear end is right in the center of the seat, and your body is facing forward. Your legs are spread apart, and your feet and knees are braced against the boat.

If you lean too far to one side, you can upset the balance of the boat. If you slouch over or lean back too far, you won't be able to get all the power and control you need to operate the boat.

As with other sports, you want to build endurance, work on muscle strength, and increase stamina. A half hour of hard, consistent paddling is very good exercise. If you are paddling correctly, you will be working your arms, shoulders, back, legs, and feet to get a well-rounded workout. Even loading and unloading your boat and carrying it to the shoreline are part of the workout.

Paddling for exercise is always a good reason to grab a boat and head to the water. And this practice will help you keep good posture, even when you're not on the water!

PADDLING STROKES

Pulling your paddle through the water is called a **stroke**. Different strokes have names that help tell what they do. For example, a **forward stroke** means you use the paddle to move forward.

A **back stroke** is used to move the boat backward. A **sweep stroke** is used to turn the boat. There are times when you might combine strokes. For example, if you are paddling backward and have to turn the boat slightly to one side, you could use a sweeping back stroke. You can even use what's called a **scull stroke** to help you move the canoe or kayak sideways through the water!

Many strokes have the same name when canoeing or kayaking but are done differently because of the difference in the paddle and the design of the boat.

START SCULL STROKE

FINISH SCULL STROKE

To get the most out of your stroke, use the muscles in your shoulders and back (called your torso area). Instead of pulling straight back with your arms only, turn your body slightly and let your torso pull, too. You will have a more powerful stroke, be able to paddle for a longer time, and get a better workout if you use your whole upper body instead of just your arms.

Another important part of good paddling technique is to use the foot braces when you paddle. Pushing against them spreads out the power of your stroke. That will help you paddle easier and longer.

For canoeing, the paddle is pulled at a right angle to the surface of the water. Be sure your canoe paddle is the right length so you get the most out of each stroke. The blade should be completely in the water, right up to the throat. If the paddle is too short, part of the blade will be sticking out of the water. If it's too long, the whole paddle and some of the shaft will completely be underwater.

Sometimes you will need to switch sides with your paddle to keep your canoe moving straight ahead. This is especially true in a one-person canoe. It takes practice to take your paddle out of the water on one side and then place it back in the water on the other side. If your switch is smooth, your canoe will continue moving in a straight line.

LOW POSITION

HIGH POSITION

For kayaking, keep your paddle low to the water if you want a relaxing, long stroke. This type of paddling is also good for covering great distances without getting tired. If you want more speed and quick power, use a higher and shorter stroke. Both work best if you keep good posture.

MANEUVERING THE BOAT

Besides basic paddling, you may need to steer your canoe or kayak around rocks or through rapids. A large wave could tip your canoe or capsize your kayak. Practicing what to do in those situations will help you be safe in an emergency.

If your canoe or kayak is upset and you are dumped into the water, you need to know how to get back into it. This can be fun to practice on a hot day, when you like to be in the water anyway.

If your kayak turns over and your spray skirt is snug around you (like the one in the photo below), it can help hold you inside the cockpit. You use your paddle to help you get upright again. This maneuver is called a **sweep roll.** Be sure to hold your breath when you are underwater practicing this maneuver. You may also want to wear nose plugs!

PRACTICE CAPSIZING

When practicing what to do if your boat capsizes, make sure another boater is there to help you if you need it. Also let them know you will be practicing the maneuvers so you don't scare them!

HOW DO I PREPARE FOR A TRIP?

A big part of planning a canoe or kayak trip is to pack as much, or as little, **gear** as you will need. Then you stow it in places that will keep your boat in **balance** and easy to **maneuver.**

There will be days when you paddle around a **small bay,** or a **country lake,** or take a short trip down a **local river.** Other adventures will take you on long journeys in remote areas far from towns and roads.

Both types of trips require **planning.**

RANGER RICK
NATIONAL WILDLIFE FEDERATION

USING DRY BAGS

Even a small canoe or kayak can carry a large amount of gear. The trick is to know how to pack it into the boat so all your equipment is dry, convenient to get to when you need it, and packed just right so it doesn't move around or upset the balance of your boat when you are paddling.

A very handy piece of gear is a **dry bag,** or **stuff sack.** Dry bags come in a variety of sizes to let you store practically anything: your clothes, a sleeping bag, your tent, camera, cell phone, flashlight, food, and cooking gear. If it's something you want to keep from getting wet, put it in a dry bag!

Most dry bags are made of waterproof nylon. Others are made of fabric that is coated with a special plastic that makes the cloth waterproof. Sometimes the cloth-coated bags crack where the bag is repeatedly folded or creased. They don't last as long as the nylon bags. A good dry bag seals so tightly that it locks in the air, keeps water out, and continues to protect your gear even if it falls into the water.

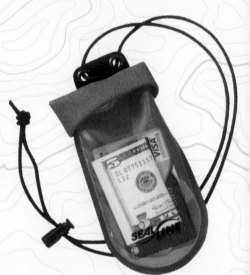

Dry bags come in a variety of colors, and some are clear so you can see what's inside.

Paddlers who take trips for several days need to carry a lot of food. Some paddlers put all the food used to make only their breakfasts in the same color of dry bag. Others put all the food for one day's worth of meals in the same bag. This makes it easier to unload your boat (especially a kayak) when you have lots of bags stuffed inside. Some dry bags serve two purposes. They are often shaped like the bow or stern of the boat, which allows them to be used to store gear in those small areas. And, because they have trapped air inside, they can double as extra flotation.

TRIMMING YOUR BOAT

Placing gear in your canoe or kayak so it doesn't lean to one side or dip in the front or back is called **trimming your boat.** When you stow your gear in the boat, you want to make sure it doesn't shift around. The heaviest pieces should be packed along the center line of the boat and usually near the middle of the boat (in a canoe) or near the paddler (in a kayak).

Once you start paddling, you can tell if your canoe or kayak is trimmed properly. If it tips to one side or the bow seems to be too low or too high in the water, you will have to shift gear around to balance the boat.

There are times when you might make the bow or stern lower or higher by placing gear differently. If the wind is blowing strongly from the front of the boat, you might want to make the bow lower going into the wind by putting slightly more weight toward the front. In a kayak, you might want the stern of the boat lower in the water if seas are pushing you from behind. By carefully packing your boat, you can usually make these changes quickly and safely.

MAKING A FLOAT PLAN

A float plan is like a schedule of where you are going and how long you plan to be gone. You leave it behind so others know when to expect you back or know where to look for you if you don't come back on schedule.

Just telling a friend that you and a buddy are going to canoe down a river and camp on a certain island for the weekend is a simple float plan. A more detailed plan is important when you are going to be gone for a longer time, be farther from home, or perhaps be paddling in a new or remote area.

A good float plan lists everyone in the group. It lists the kinds of boats everyone has and even what color they are. It also tells where you plan to paddle and how long you will stay at each place.

Of course, the plan is no good if you change your mind and go someplace else. If that happens, you should tell someone where you are headed. It could be a ranger, outfitter, or other paddlers you meet along the route.

MY PADDLING FLOAT PLAN

DATE: _____

WHO IS PADDLING:

_____

_____

_____

WHERE WE ARE GOING:

FROM _____

_____

_____

TO _____

_____

_____

START TIME

STOP TIME

EMERGENCY PHONE NUMBERS:

(_ _ _) _ _ _ - _ _ _ _

(_ _ _) _ _ _ - _ _ _ _

(_ _ _) _ _ _ - _ _ _ _

MY NAME:

_____

One important reason for having a float plan is so that someone knows where to find you if you get into trouble. The weather can turn bad and keep you from returning on time. Someone may become ill or get hurt and can't travel. You may be stuck somewhere and run out of food. It will be good to know that someone back home is expecting you and will use the float plan to find you.

When you are away from home, you can give a copy of your float plan to the harbormaster at the harbor where you launch your trip. You can give it to a forest or camp ranger, too. You can even tape it to the window of your car so someone can find it if they are looking for you.

BEFORE YOU PACK

Planning ahead will make any trip more fun and enjoyable. Here are a few questions about what to bring on a canoe or kayak trip.

- Will there be beautiful scenery to photograph?

- Should you bring binoculars to watch the wildlife?

- Will your cell phone work in case of an emergency?

- Will you be gone long enough to need extra batteries for your flashlight, camera, or cell phone?

- What about a first-aid kit or special medicine for someone in your group?

- Will the weather be changing so you will need special or extra clothing?

- What will you want to bring to entertain yourself (a book, a journal, games, etc.) while relaxing in camp?

WHERE CAN I GO?

You may know that the Earth is often called the **water planet** because so much of it is covered by **oceans.** And even on the continents there are more **lakes** than land in some places.

There are plenty of city, county, and national **parks;** ocean waters with coves, bays, and islands to **explore;** rivers, lakes, and even glacial bays where you can go **paddling.** You don't have to go very far, no matter where you **live**, to find a **great place** to **paddle.**

PARKS

City and county parks with lakes or rivers are excellent places to learn how to paddle. As you get more experience you can venture out into your region to find more and more water to explore.

Many state and national parks have water trails for paddling from campsite to campsite on different lakes or down a river running through the park. Some areas have chains of lakes that are all connected to one another by narrow rivers or channels.

Lake McDonald in Glacier National Park, Montana

Not all of these parks will have paddling opportunities, but many do. Some of these areas have clubs and organizations that offer lessons and special events. They may also have rental boats.

Many states and provinces have national parks, shown on this map with a ⛰ symbol. See the lists on pages 92 and 93 for their names and locations. Find the parks close to you and see if they have any areas where you can paddle.

OCEAN WATERS

The oceans around the world offer paddlers endless miles of beaches with protective coves and bays or islands to explore.

PACIFIC

The Pacific Northwest region includes the coasts of Washington, Oregon, and British Columbia. It has many rapid-flowing rivers for whitewater canoeing and kayaking. The mountain lakes are especially good for canoeing. **Vancouver Island** in Canada and **Puget Sound** in Washington have hundreds of bays to paddle. A big thrill for paddlers in this region is the chance to see a whale or sea lions.

The coast of California has many sandy beaches for launching a kayak, including the **Channel Islands National Park.**

Channel Islands National Park, California

The **Hawaiian Islands** and others throughout the South Pacific are great for sea kayaking around islands, coral reefs, and atolls in sparkling clear, warm waters.

GULF OF MEXICO

The warm waters of the Gulf of Mexico are very inviting to kayakers. You will find many long stretches of beaches, plus miles of mangrove forests along Florida's southern tip. In the Gulf of Mexico, you will find many places to canoe, including rivers with clear springs.

ATLANTIC

All along the Atlantic Coast are bays, estuaries, and other bodies of water that are perfect for kayaking and canoeing. Even in the ocean you can find protected areas where the waves are small and the water is gentle. Exploring the shoreline in a boat is a wonderful way to see marine animals.

Acadia National Park, Maine

Maine is popular for kayakers because of its rugged coastline. **Acadia National Park** is a favorite place for kayakers because of all the islands and tiny bays to explore.

INTERIOR WATERS

Many states and provinces in North America have exciting areas for canoeing and kayaking. Much of the kayaking is whitewater, but any lake you canoe in, you can paddle your kayak, too. Large lakes even have outfitters to help you get the gear you need to enjoy a day or a week of paddling.

Great Smoky Mountains National Park, Tennessee

EASTERN REGION

In many provinces and states, such as Quebec, Virginia, the Carolinas, Kentucky, and Tennessee, you can find fast rivers for whitewater kayaking or canoeing.

THE GREAT LAKES

The biggest freshwater lakes in the world offer some of the best paddling in all of North America. Many of the northern bays have rocky shorelines with towering cliffs. These lakes can be as cold and raging as the ocean, so you need to be a good paddler!

Isle Royale National Park is located in Lake Superior. It has many narrow passages and long bays to explore. You can camp each day in a new spot as you travel around the wilderness island.

The **Apostle Islands** on Wisconsin's Lake Superior shoreline are also a very popular for paddlers. There are several islands that have a network of caves right on the water. You can paddle into these huge openings and travel through tunnel-like spaces. There are campsites on several islands.

There is also a water trail that runs along Minnesota's north shore of Lake Superior, from the town of Two Harbors to the Canadian border. Special campsites and take-out spots at some of Minnesota's prettiest state parks are all part of this new route.

THE MIDWEST

The northernmost part of the Midwest has some of the best canoe country in America. There are also many wonderful places in the central part of the United States, some more than 500 miles (800 km) from the nearest ocean, where you can enjoy fantastic paddling.

For example, the **Boundary Waters Canoe Area Wilderness** (BWCAW) and **Voyageurs National Park** are known for great canoeing. There are thousands of lakes and nearly as many miles of rivers joined together to form routes for paddlers—from young beginners to old pros. There are tiny islands you can camp on, waterfalls to explore, and lakes of all sizes to watch wildlife or catch fish.

Boundary Waters Canoe Area Wilderness, Minnesota

Boundary Waters Canoe Area Wilderness, Minnesota

The **Mississippi River** also has areas along the main river channel called **sloughs** where you can paddle into remote sections that are rich in wildlife. Both canoes and kayaks work well in these areas.

Canoeists find many exciting rivers in this region, too. The **St. Croix** and **Namekogan** flow out of Wisconsin. Their waters eventually join with the Mississippi River. You can take day trips or extended journeys down most of these rivers.

Many states have rivers that are so special for paddling that they are designated as wild and scenic rivers. The **Current River** in central Missouri is a great example.

ALASKA

From glacial bays to chains of lakes, Alaska has it all. Several regions in Alaska offer spectacular kayaking opportunities.

SOUTHEAST REGION

This area, known as the panhandle, includes the towns of Ketchikan, Wrangell, and others. Coastal kayaking is popular here because of all the remote bays and long fjord-like waterways that cut deep into the Alaska coastline. A favorite kayaking destination is **Misty Fjords National Monument. Glacier Bay National Park** also offers paddlers hundreds of remote bays tucked into snow-covered mountains.

The area around Sitka and Juneau is popular, too. There are even hot springs where you can relax in the warmth of these natural hot pools.

Shoup Bay State Marine Park, Valdez, Alaska

PRINCE WILLIAM SOUND

Between the cities of Whittier on the west and Valdez on the east lies 100 miles (161 km) of ocean with remote islands, towering mountains, and glaciers, including Shoup Glacier, which you can see from **Shoup Bay State Marine Park.**

Aialik Bay, Alaska

KENAI PENINSULA

Homer and Seward offer many coastal opportunities for kayaking. **Kenai Fjords National Park,** south of Seward, is renowned for its wildlife viewing and scenery. It's accessible by floatplane from both cities.

KODIAK ISLANDS

Just south of the Kenai Peninsula is the island of Kodiak. Its deeply cut bays make it a wonderful place for kayaking. You have a great opportunity to see huge coastal brown bears going after spawning salmon. **Shuyak Island State Park** is a popular destination for guided kayaking trips.

OTHER AREAS

There are a couple of really good places to canoe, too. The **Swanson River** area by Soldotna has miles of river routes through moose country. **Wood-Tikchik State Park** has a series of remote lakes all connected together.

ALL AROUND THE WORLD

Sea kayaking has become so popular there is only one continent where you can't paddle it—the ice continent of Antarctica. The rest of the world, from the largest countries to the smallest ocean islands, have places to paddle. Here are a few popular places among kayakers.

Corsica, France

MEXICO AND CENTRAL AMERICA

In Mexico, there are two major regions where kayaking is very popular. One area just south of California is Baja. There kayakers can enjoy clear water in a desert environment while watching gray whales gather with their young. Across the country on the Caribbean/Gulf of Mexico side is the state of Yucatán. Here you can paddle the coastline scouting out Mayan ruins and flamingos.

Costa Rica, Belize and Honduras offer fantastic kayaking in warm, swimming-pool-clear waters. Some of the world's longest coral reefs are here. There are also small, sandy islands that are perfect places to paddle to so you can swim with rainbow-colored fish.

NORTHERN EUROPE

In Britain, sea kayaking is called sea canoeing. Bays in Scotland and chains of islands and canals farther south make kayaking and inland canoeing very popular. There are guided kayak tours along the coast of Scandinavia, too, from Norway to Sweden to Finland.

GREECE

Touring companies make it easy for paddlers to visit exotic places. Paddling around the islands of Greece is just one example. The company provides all the paddling gear you need to have a great sea kayaking adventure.

You can kayak almost anywhere in the world. The south of Thailand has many amazing sea kayaking areas.

WHAT ELSE CAN I DO?

Paddling can include just the feeling of the **breeze as you cruise** along a smooth surface, or it can be the **mist in your face** as you race through a rapids or charge into the waves and wind.

Sometimes **your boat** is simply a way to **enjoy the outdoors** in another way. It is a way to get to a place you can't walk to or otherwise experience.

Here are a few examples of **other activities** you can use your boat to enjoy.

EXPLORING

Because canoes and kayaks are so small and can move through the water so quietly, they are excellent boats for exploring. They both can be paddled in very shallow water so they can go where practically no other craft of the same size is able to venture.

Becoming a skilled paddler means learning how to judge different types of waters (rivers, lakes, ponds, channels, reservoirs, etc.) to make sure they are safe for paddling and exploring. When exploring, always make sure it is safe, and stay aware of your surroundings.

In some areas of North America, the melting of winter snows means that the backwaters of many rivers overflow, flooding wooded areas along the banks. Sometimes the flooding just covers the low woodlands in a few feet of water, making it possible to paddle through trees in the spring that you may be able to hike through later on.

WILDLIFE WATCHING

One of the coolest things about paddling is seeing birds and other wildlife. The kayak and canoe make it easy to reach remote areas of lakes and rivers and deep into protected bays where wildlife lives. On foot, people usually make noise and scare animals away, but on the water it is easier to be quiet and see more wildlife. You must be very careful to stay far enough away so you don't disturb them or bring danger to yourself. As your balance improves, you will be able to sit still for long periods of time to watch how animals live in the wild.

On oceans, it's usually possible to find offshore islands that are homes to many of the seabirds in an area. On lakes, loons are usually found in quiet areas.

Seals and sea lions like to climb up on rocks and warm themselves in the sun. These areas are called haul outs, and you can usually hear the animals before you see them. Your kayak is the perfect boat to use as an observation platform from which to enjoy their antics.

Loons

Moose

California sea lions

Sometimes while paddling along back bays, you might see foxes, deer, or otters walking along the beach. And don't forget to look up in the sky while paddling, either. You might catch a glimpse of an eagle soaring overhead or terns and other seabirds looking for food.

Humpback whale

A special treat when paddling on the ocean is a chance to see a whale. You may see them leap from the water with bodies the size of a school bus!

On lakes and rivers, it is possible to see even more animals than you might see from shore. An hour before sunset, you may catch a moose grazing in the reeds. Sometimes deer come down to the water's edge to drink. Raccoons may also be nearby.

Shorebirds are always a joy to watch, and from a canoe or kayak, you can float through the shallow waters where many of these birds look for food during the day. Sometimes you can watch a large egret or heron, too. In some parts of North America, it's common to see beavers, muskrats, or even otters swimming across a pond or lake. In warm water, you can add frogs, snakes, and turtles to the list of animals you might see while paddling.

Canada geese

Bald eagle

FISHING AND CAMPING

Fishing from a canoe or kayak is like any other kind of fishing, except these are smaller boats. You must bring only the gear you will need. Many paddlers add a fishing rod holder to their boat so they have a place to keep their rod handy.

In a canoe, your tackle box can fit under your seat. In a kayak, even without a spray skirt, you don't have a lot of space to keep your gear handy. One type of kayak that is very popular is called a Sit-On-Top kayak. Instead of sitting down inside the kayak, the paddler of an SOT sits in a seat on top of the boat. There is a special well for the paddler's heels. These boats look like fat, thick surfboards. You use a regular kayak paddle to move yourself through the water.

Paddling is a great way to find new places to camp, or come ashore and relax. You can plan picnics and other shore snack breaks by carrying a small camp stove and small, soft-sided coolers made especially for packing in a canoe or kayak.

Wherever you paddle, remember: **Be safe and have fun!**

APPENDIX

WHEN I GET HOME

As soon as you get home, clean your boat so it will be ready for your next paddling adventure. If you take care of your equipment, it will last for many years.

BOAT CARE

Wash off any mud, sand, and dry saltwater crystals from the outside of your canoe or kayak. Pay special attention to the rudder, deck, and cockpit areas of a kayak. Clean off all weeds so you don't spread them to another area. Be sure to rinse out the inside of your boat, too.

If you practice paddling in a swimming pool, be sure to rinse your boat right after the session. After time, the chemicals in pool water may damage the boat.

GEAR STORAGE

Rinse off zippers on life jackets and boots and anything else on your boat or gear that snaps, zips, or clips together. Be sure everything is completely dry before you put it away.

If you use a two-piece paddle, take it apart and rinse off the ends. Make sure they are dry before you put them back together.

For kayaks, be sure to follow the manufacturer's directions to lubricate the moving parts so they continue to work well.

BOAT STORAGE

After a good cleaning, canoes and kayaks can be stored sitting on one of their sides, on their top or bottom, or hanging from straps. It's also important to make sure nothing will fall on the boat if it's stored outside. If you store your boat on the ground, be sure it doesn't move around. That could accidentally poke a hole in the side.

A canoe stored on a rack or sawhorse should rest on the section of the gunwale where the thwarts are connected. A kayak stored on a rack or sawhorse should rest on the bulkheads.

If you are hanging a boat, make sure the straps are hooked to a strong point on the ceiling or wall. They should wrap around the hull where the thwarts are on the canoe, or where the bulkheads are on the kayak.

You can place a tarp or other covering over the boat. Make sure no water will get in. Some kayakers prefer to use just a cockpit cover to keep out water, dirt, and animals.

NATIONAL PARKS

You can learn more information about the U.S. National Parks listed below, plus all the parks in your state, by visiting the National Park Service website: **www.nps.gov.**

Acadia, ME

Arches, UT

Badlands, SD

Big Bend, TX

Biscayne, FL

Black Canyon of the Gunnison, CO

Bryce Canyon, UT

Canyonlands, UT

Capitol Reef, UT

Carlsbad Caverns, NM

Channel Islands, CA

Congaree, SC

Crater Lake, OR

Cuyahoga Valley, OH

Death Valley, CA

Denali, AK

Dry Tortugas, FL

Everglades, FL

Gates of the Arctic, AK

Glacier, MT

Glacier Bay, AK

Grand Canyon, AZ

Grand Teton, WY

Great Basin, NV

Great Sand Dunes, CO

Great Smoky Mountains, NC, TN

Guadalupe Mountains, TX

Haleakala, HI

Hawaii Volcanoes, HI

Hot Springs, AR

Isle Royale, MI

Joshua Tree, CA

Katmai, AK

Kenai Fjords, AK

King Canyon, CA

Kobuk Valley, AK

Lake Clark, AK

Lassen Volcanic, CA

Mammoth Cave, KY

Mesa Verde, CO

Mount Rainier, WA

North Cascades, WA

Olympic, WA

Petrified Forest, AZ

Pinnacles, CA

Redwood, CA

Rocky Mountain, CO

Saguaro, AZ

Sequoia, CA

Shenandoah, VA

Theodore Roosevelt, ND

Voyageurs, MN

Wind Cave, SD

Wrangell—St. Elias, AK

Yellowstone, ID, MT, WY

Yosemite, CA

Zion, UT

You can learn more information about the Canadian National Parks listed below, by visiting the Parks Canada website: **www.pc.gc.ca.**

Aulavik, NT

Auyuittuq, NU

Banff, AB

Bruce Peninsula, ON

Cape Breton Highlands, NS

Elk Island, AB

Fathom Five, ON

Forillon, QC

Fundy, NB

Georgian Bay Islands, ON

Glacier, BC

Grasslands, SK

Gros Morne, NL

Gulf Islands, BC

Gwaii Haanas, BC

Ivvavik, YT

Jasper, AB

Kejimkujik, NS

Kluane, YT

Kootenay, BC

Kouchibouguac, NB

La Mauricie, QC

Mingan Archipelago, QC

Mount Revelstoke, BC

Nahanni, NT

Pacific Rim, BC

Point Pelee, ON

Prince Albert, SK

Prince Edward Island, PE

Pukaskwa, ON

Qausuittuq, NV

Quttinirpaag, NV

Riding Mountain, MB

Rogue Park, ON

Sable Island, NS

Jaquenay—St. Lawrence, QC

Saint Lawrence Islands, ON

Sirmilik, NUN

Terra Nova, NF

Thousand Islands, ON

Torngat Mountains, NL

Tuktut Nogait, NT

Ukkusiksalik, NU

Vuntut, YT

Wapusk, MB

Waterton Lakes, AB

Wood Buffalo, AB, NT

Yoho, BC

INDEX

A
Alaska, 76–77
Atlantic Ocean, 71

B
Beaver tail
    paddle, 40
Bent-shaft
    paddle, 40
Blade, 38–42, 51
Bow, 8, 10, 17, 19, 59, 61
Bulkhead, 18

C
Camping, 37, 62, 65, 68,
    73–74, 88
Canoes, 6–15
Centerline, 60
Central America, 78
Clothing and
    Accessories,
    34–36
Coaming, 17, 32
Cockpit, 17–19, 22–23, 54
Compartment, 18

D
Deck, 17–19, 21, 25, 32, 43
Dry bag, 37, 58-59

E
Eastern North America,
    72–73

Exploring, 82

F
Fishing, 22–23, 27, 74, 78,
    88
Float plan, 62–64
Foot brace, 51

G
Gloves, 35–36
Great Lakes, The, 73
Greece, 79
Greenland paddle, 41
Grip, 25, 27, 38–39
Gulf of Mexico, 69
Gunwale, 8

H
Hat, 35–36
Hatch, 18
High-volume kayak, 20

J
Jacket, 34

K
Kayaks, 16–23
Keel, 10–11, 17

L
Life jacket, 26, 30–33
Lines, 17, 32

M
Midsection, 8
Midwest, The, 74–75

N
Northern Europe, 79

P
Pacific Ocean, 70
Paddles, 38–43
Paddling strokes, 48–53
Pants, 34
Parks, 68–69
Pedal, 18–19
PFD (personal
    flotation device), 26,
    30–33

Pogie, 36
Portage, 8
Posture, 46

R
Recreational
    kayak, 22
Rocker, 10, 25
Rudder, 19

S
Seats, 9
Shaft, 38–40, 51
Sit-On-Top kayak, 23, 88
Skeg, 19
Spray skirt, 17, 23, 54
Stand-up paddleboards,
    24–27
Stem, 10
Stern, 8, 10, 17, 19, 59, 61
Stuff sack, (see dry bag)
Sweep roll, 54
Sweep stroke, 48

T
Throat, 38–39, 41, 51
Thwart, 8
Tip, 38–39
Torso, 49
Track, 10, 15, 20, 23, 25, 27
Trimming your boat, 60–61
Tumblehome, 15

W
Whitewater kayak, 10, 20,
    23
Wildlife watching, 84–87

Y
Yoke, 8

AUTHOR

Tom Watson reviews and field-tests watercraft, camping, and survival products. He spent five years as a **Kodiak Island Search & Rescue member** and more than 12 years as a **guide and outfitter in Alaska.** Tom is also the author of several books, including **How to Think Like a Survivor: A Guide for Wilderness Emergencies.** He lives in Owatonna, Minnesota.

NATIONAL WILDLIFE FEDERATION NATURALIST

David Mizejewski is a naturalist, author, and television host. As a wildlife expert, he appears on many television and radio shows, from **Today** to **NPR** and **Conan,** and is a **Nat Geo WILD** host. A lifelong nature-lover, David spent his youth exploring the woods, fields, and wetlands, observing and learning all about the natural world around us. He lives in Washington, DC.